Father James Ra[...]

    May he who has begun
this good work in you
continue to perfect it
until the day of Christ Jesus.

           Frank Fawcett
           27 May 1965

IN PRAISE OF ST. PAUL

IN PRAISE
OF SAINT PAUL

BY

St. John Chrysostom

TRANSLATED BY

Rev. Thomas Halton, Ph.D.

THE CATHOLIC UNIVERSITY OF AMERICA

WASHINGTON, D.C.

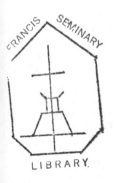

ST. PAUL EDITIONS

NIHIL OBSTAT:

Rt. Rev. Matthew P. Stapleton
Diocesan Censor

IMPRIMATUR:

✝ Richard Cardinal Cushing
Archbishop of Boston

Oct. 22, 1963

Library of Congress Catalog Card number: 63-14468

Printed by the *Daughters of St. Paul*
50 St. Paul's Ave., Jamaica Plain, Boston, Mass. 02130

INTRODUCTION

The Greek text used for this translation of St. John Chrysostom's seven panegyrics *In Praise of St. Paul* is that found in Migne, *Patrologia Graeca*, (Paris, 1862), vol. 50, cols. 473-514. The complete seven sermons have not been translated into English before the present work; a translation of the seventh sermon, however, will be found, with some minor differences, in Stephen Neill, *Chrysostom and His Message* (World Christian Books, New York, 1963).

St. John Chrysostom has left us as many as 250 homilies on the Epistles of St. Paul (Migne, vols. 60-63), which are generally considered to be the finest commentary ever written on the Epistles of the Apostle of the Gentiles. The present series of panegyrics also testifies to his close knowledge of St. Paul's writings as well as to his deep admiration and attachment to Paul's many virtues. Reading them we can easily see what he meant in the introduction to his commentary on the Epistle to the Romans: "As often as I hear the Epistles of St. Paul read, twice a week, or often three or four times, I rejoice each time over this spiritual trumpet, and I exult and am kindled with holy desires, when I hear the voice which is to me so dear and familiar, and then I imagine that I see him living before me, and that I hear him speak."

It seems certain from references in Sermon Four (p. 51) to Julian and the Shrine of Apollo at Daphne, a suburb of Antioch, that these panegyrics were preached at Antioch sometime during Chrysostom's twelve-year stay there after his ordination (386-398 A.D.).

Among recent books on St. John Chrysostom the following are recommended for further study: Baur, *John Chrysostom and His Time* (tr. Sr. M. Gonzaga), 2 vols. (Newman Press, Westminster, Md., 1959, 1960), *St. John Chrysostom: Baptismal Instructions,* tr. P. W. Harkins (Ancient Christian Writers, No. 31, Newman Press, 1963), and Neill, *Chrysostom and His Message* (Association Press, New York, 1963). Complete bibliographies on St. John Chrysostom and his copious works will be found in Quasten, Patrology, vol. 3, (Westminster, Md., 1960), 424-82.

CONTENTS

Sermon I

PAUL POSSESSED THE FULLNESS
OF ALL BLESSINGS

He was greater than Abel, Noah, Abraham, Isaac, Jacob,
Joseph, Job, Moses, David, Elias, John the Baptist,
the angels.

13

One could rightly describe the soul of St. Paul as a seedbed of virtue and a spiritual paradise. For grace already flourished deeply in him and he constantly tended his soul to fit it for the growth and development of grace. When he became a vase of election and had thoroughly purified himself, he received a liberal infusion of the Holy Spirit. And so he became for us the source of many miraculous rivers, not just the four that originate in Paradise but numerous others running daily for each one of us, irrigating not the earth but the souls of men and causing them to sprout forth virtues.

What words will adequately describe this man's goodness? Or what tongue can adequately chant his praises? When one soul possesses all, human virtues, I should say more than all, and not only human but angelic virtues, how can we hope to compose an encomium? Yet we must not on that account remain silent, but rather on that very account we must speak. For this is the greatest kind of encomium: When the greatness of the accomplishments surpasses the attempt, however eloquent, at description, and to find our efforts defeated is more gratifying than to score any number of successes. Where should we start, then, in our praises? Where else but from the point that Paul possesses the fulness of all bless-

ings? Any nobility displayed by prophets, or
patriarchs, or the just, or the apostles, or martyrs,
Paul has in a superabundant degree.

Mark this. Abel, you say, offered sacrifice
and for this he was proclaimed.[1] But if you examine the sacrifice of Paul it will be seen to surpass Abel's as much as the heavens surpass the
earth. You ask what I mean? Simply this, that Paul
made a complete sacrifice of himself every day,
and his oblation was two-fold: first, he died
daily, [2] and secondly, he was always bearing about
in his body the death of Jesus. [3] For he constantly
faced dangers and was willing to accept martyr-
dom. By mortifying his body he virtually became
a sacrificial offering, in fact more than a sacrifice.
For it was not cattle and sheep that he offered but
his own flesh and blood in this two-fold daily sacrifice. Accordingly he made bold to say *I am
already being poured out in sacrifice* (2 Tim. 4:5),
calling his own blood an immolation. And he was
not satisfied with these sacrifices. After he had
a complete oblation of himself, he desired to make
an oblation of the whole world, earth and sea,
Greek and barbarian, every land encompassed by
the sky, this land which he traversed as if he were
a creature on wings, and not just as a mere
traveler. He plucked out the thorns of sin.on the
way, sowed everywhere the word of religion,

drove out error, restored truth, made angels of
men, or rather changed men from devils into
angels. And so, as he was about to leave behind
all these hardships and the thick of the fight he
said, by way of consolation to his disciples: *But
even if I am made the libation for the sacrifice and
service of your faith, I joy and rejoice with you.
And in the same way do you also joy and rejoice
with me.* (Phil. 2:17-18). What sacrifice, then,
could equal this sacrifice which Paul offered,
immolating it with the sword of the spirit and
offering it on the altar raised high above the
heavens.

Abel, you say, was laid low and treacherously
slain by his brother.[4] This magnified his greatness.
But I will count up innumerable deaths, a death
for every day the blessed Paul preached. If you
must know sacrifice reaching to the very limits,
Abel was slain by his brother who had not been
injured nor conferred any benefits; Paul was put
to death by those whom he had tried to rescue
from every kind of evil and for whom he had endured every kind of suffering.

Noah, you say, was a just man, perfect in his
generation,[5] and unique among mankind. But
Paul was truly unique. Noah merely saved himself and his children. But Paul, when a fierce
flood lashed the earth, rescued not just two or

three or five relations, but the whole world from
imminent shipwreck, not by fitting together
planks to make an ark, but by working on tablets
instead of planks. His ark was not such as to be
carried around in one place since it extended to
the ends of the earth, and in it he carried all peoples down to the present time. For he made it to
hold the multitude to be saved, admitting those
more foolish than the dumb animals, and making
them imitate the powers above. This proved the
superiority of his ark. For Noah's received a ra-
ven, [6] took in a wolf but did not change its savage
nature. Paul, on the other hand, changed wolves
into sheep, and hawks and daws into doves. He
replaced the irrational and savage nature of man
with the gentleness of the Spirit, and his ark still
remains afloat and has not perished. The storm of
wickedness could not loosen its planks; instead, it
surmounted the storm and restored calm. And
why not? For its planks were greased not with
asphalt and pitch, [7] but with the Holy Spirit.

All men, you say, admire Abraham for quitting home and fatherland, friends and relatives,
when he heard the command, *Abraham, depart
from your country and your relatives* (Gen. 12:1).
God ordered it and that meant everything to him.
We admire him, too. But does this make him
Paul's equal? Paul left not just fatherland, home,

and relatives, but the world itself for the sake of Jesus, or rather I should say heaven itself. He despised the heaven of heavens and sought just one thing, the love of Jesus. Listen to his own clear words on this matter: *nor things present, nor things to come, nor height, nor depth, will be able to separate us from the love of God* (Rom. 8:38-39). Abraham, you say, risked dangers and rescued his nephew [8] from the barbarians. But Paul rescued, not just his nephew, not three or four cities, but the whole world and not just from barbarians, but from the hands of the devil himself, enduring countless dangers daily, and by his own several deaths achieving salvation for others. To sacrifice his son, you say, was the crown of goodness and the garland of philosophy. But you will find Paul first in this also. For he sacrificed not his son, but himself countless times, as I have been saying.

Men marvel at Isaac for many things, chiefly his patience. For he dug wells [9] and when he was evicted from his possessions he did not quarrel, but allowed his wells to be stopped, and always moved to another place, not mustering his forces against his enemy but quitting and leaving his possessions until they satisfied their desire for injustice. Paul, when he saw not just his wells filled with earth but his body assailed by stones, did not quit like this man, but went after those that pelted him and strove to lead them to heaven. The more the well was choked up the more he gushed forth, bursting into more rivers of endurance.

Isaac's son, Jacob, you say, is admired in scripture for his strength. [10] But what soul, however adamant, could match the endurance of Paul. He endured slavery not just for fourteen [11] years, but for a lifetime for the bride of Christ, enduring not just the heat of the day and the frost of night but countless storms of trials—the lash, stoning, fighting with wild beasts, wrestling with the sea, constant fasting day and night, exposure,[12] everywhere avoiding pitfalls, and snatching the sheep from the jaws of the devil.

Joseph, you say, was a man of temperance. [13] I am afraid it would be ridiculous to praise Paul on that score—he who crucified himself to the world, [14] who regarded as dust and ashes not just bodily beauty but everything, and was as unmoved by it as a corpse by a corpse. He so lulled the promptings of the flesh that he never succumbed to any human passion.

All men, you say, admire Job. And very properly so. For he fought a great fight and can stand comparison with Paul for his patience, his purity of life, his testimony to God, his courageous struggle with the devil, the victory in which his struggle ended. But Paul's struggle lasted not just a matter of months, but many years; he was constantly running into the mouth of the lion, wrestling with countless temptations, and proved more resilient than any rock throughout. He was reviled not just by three or four friends but by all the infidel false brethren, calumniated, spat upon and reviled.

Job's hospitality was great, and also his care for the poor. That we do not deny, but we will find that it falls as far short of Paul's as the body falls short of the soul. Job cared for the sick in body; Paul did the same for those suffering from spiritual maladies, at one time directing those spiritually lame and maimed, at another clothing the naked and exposed with the stole of philosophy.

Job's house had an open door for visitors, but Paul's soul kept an open door to the whole world and was absolutely ecumenical in its hospitality. This prompted him to say: *In us there is no lack of room for you but in your heart there is no room for us* (2 Cor. 6:12). To those in need Job was liberal from his extensive sheepfolds and herds; Paul had nothing more than his own body but he used it to minister to those in need as he exclaimed: *These hands of mine have provided for my needs and those of my companions* (Acts 20:34), feeding the hungry by the work of his body.

Worms, you say, and wounds inflicted severe, unendurable pains on Job. I agree. But if you consider the lashes St. Paul received through the years, the constant fasting, the nakedness, the chains, the imprisonment, the dangers, the schemings of his own household and outsiders, of tyrants and of the whole world, and add to this even more bitter experiences, I mean the pains endured for the fallen, the concern for all the churches, the fever which he endured for each of the scandalized, you will see, perhaps, how stout his soul was in enduring such things, stouter than iron or adamant.

Paul endured spiritually what Job suffered physically, and sorrow worse than any worms gnawed at his soul for those fallen away. Fountains of tears welled from him by day and by night, and for each soul he was in greater affliction than a woman in labor. This led him to say: *my dear children, with whom I am in labor again* (Gal. 4:19).

Whom do you name after Job as worthy of wonder? Moses, no doubt? But Paul outdid him by a long stretch. Among Moses' many great accomplishments, his crowning glory was that he chose to be erased from the Book of Life for the salvation of the Jews,[15] but he chose to perish with others while Paul chose to forfeit eternal glory for the salvation of others without involving anyone else in his own destruction. Moses fought with the Pharaoh; Paul fought with Satan every day; Moses fought for one race, Paul fought for the whole world in a struggle involving not sweat but blood flowing everywhere; he directed to salvation the habitable and the uninhabitable, the Greek and the barbarian worlds.

I could also speak of Josue and of Samuel and the other prophets. But to keep my sermon within bounds, I will merely make comparison with their more illustrious representatives. If Paul is shown superior to those who are outstanding, there can be little doubt about the others. Who, then, are outstanding among them?

Who else after these, but David, and Elias and John? Of these Elias [16] was precursor of the Lord's first coming, John [17] of His second. This explains the coupling of their names. What was David's outstanding characteristic? Undoubtedly his humility and his love of God. And who more than, in fact who as much as, Paul possessed these two qualities of soul?

What is wonderful about Elias? That he closed Heaven, and introduced drought, and rained down fire from heaven?[18] I should think not. Rather, that he was zealous for the Lord,

absolutely fired with zeal. But if you examine
Paul's zeal you will see that it is as superior as he
was to the other prophets. What could match the
zeal of his words about the glory of God: *I could
wish to be anathema myself for the sake of my
brethren, who are my kinsmen according to the
flesh* (Rom. 9:3). Therefore, when the heavens
proffered crowns and garlands to him he delayed
and dilated saying: *to stay on in the flesh is necessary for your sake* (Phil. 1:24). So he regarded neither the visible nor the intellectual
world as sufficient for the satisfaction of his love
and zeal, but sought another non-existent one to
show what he wished and desired.

John, you say, ate locusts and wild honey. [19]
Paul spent his time in the midst of the world not
in the desert, and ate not locusts and wild honey,
but was satisfied with a much more frugal table,
neglecting even the bare necessities in his zeal for
preaching. John displayed great courage, you say,
before Herod. Paul rebuked not just one or two
or three but a countless number of the same type,
in fact tyrants far worse than Herod.

It remains for us to compare Paul with the
angels. Quitting the earth, let us ascend to the
gates of Heaven. Let no one say that our words
are overdaring. If Scripture called John an angel,

and the priests, why wonder if we claim Paul's superiority to them all in these virtues? What constitutes the greatness of the angels? Their absolute obedience to God. That is what David admired in them: *powerful in virtue, obeying his word* (Ps. 102:20). But Paul's obedience cannot be matched even by countless incorporeal beings. What makes them blessed is their obedience to God's commands and their refusal ever to disobey. Paul did that with absolute fidelity. He fulfilled God's word, and also His commands. Not just His commands but more, as he reveals, saying: *What then is my reward? That preaching the gospel, I deliver the gospel of Christ without charge* (1 Cor. 9:18).

What else does the prophet see worthy of admiration in the angels? *Who makes the winds angels, his ministers flames of fire* (Ps. 103:4). This, too, we can find in Paul. Like fire and wind, he traversed the world and cleansed it as he went. But he did not, you say, possess heaven. That makes it all the more remarkable, that while still on earth, in a mortal body, he showed such strength in combatting incorporeal powers.

How blameworthy we would be, if we should not strive to imitate in particular a man who combined all good qualities in a single person. Let

us revolve these considerations in our minds, and
escape blame; let us strive to match his zeal so that
we can share in the same blessings, by the grace
and loving kindness of our Lord, Jesus Christ, to
whom be glory and power, now and forever,
Amen.

Sermon II

ST. PAUL, OUTSTANDING EXAMPLE
OF THE POSSIBILITIES
OF HUMAN NATURE FOR VIRTUE

The love of Christ was the source of all his strivings and
his whole pleasure—His one ambition was to save souls—
Angelic in his purity and resolute in his determination—
All can share in his achievement.

St. Paul was the noblest of men and the most outstanding example of the nobility of human nature and of its possibilities for virtue. By speaking up for the Master and exhorting us to virtue he completely refutes those who find fault with human nature, seals the lips of those who make slanderous charges, and shows that little divides angels from men if they are willing to perfect themselves.

Paul's nature was no different from ours. His soul was no different. He was an inhabitant of no different world. In the same world, the same country, with the same laws and customs, he surpassed in virtue all men, present and past. Where now are those who protest that virtue is difficult and vice all too easy? This man refutes them with his words: *For our present light affliction prepares for us an eternal weight of glory that is beyond all measure* (2 Cor. 4:17). If his tribulations are light, how much more so ours, which are pleasures by comparison.

The fact that in the excess of his zeal he did not feel the pains involved in being virtuous is not the only marvelous thing about him. There is also the fact that he had no ulterior motive in his virtue. We are reluctant to endure pains to acquire virtue even when rewards are on offer, but he lovingly embraced it even without rewards and endured with all meekness whatever seemed to stand in the way of virtue. He did not chafe at bodily weakness, or pressure of engagements, or the tyranny of habit, or anything else. Yet his responsibilities exceeded those of generals or earthly kings. Nonetheless he increased daily in virtue; increasing the threats of danger only served to increase his zeal. He tells us as much in the words: *forgetting what is behind, I strain to what is before* (Phil. 3:13). When death was imminent he called them to share in this pleasure saying: *joy and rejoice with me* (Phil. 2:18) and he exulted in danger, injury, and every opprobrium. Writing to the Corinthians he says: *wherefore I am satisfied with infirmities, with insults, with hardships* (2 Cor. 12:10). He called these the arms of justice, showing that they were a fruitful source of good to him, and that he was invincible to his enemies. Though beaten, and abused, and reviled, as if in triumphal procession he erected many earthly trophies, rejoiced and offered thanks to God, saying: *thanks be to God who always leads us in triumph* (2 Cor. 2:14). To further his preaching, he was honored to accept discredit and shame, regarding death as we would life, and poverty as we would wealth, and toil as we would rest, nay far more than we would, and grief more than we would pleasure, and praying more for his enemies than others would against them. He changed the order of things, or rather, I should say it is we who change it. He merely kept it as God had decreed. For what he sought was according to nature, and what we seek is contrary to nature. The proof of this is that Paul, human though he was, sought what he did and not what we do. One thing only he feared and avoided: giving offense to God, nothing else. One pleasure only he sought: to be pleasing to God. I do not mean just present pleasure, but future pleasure as well.

Don't talk to me of cities, and peoples, and kings, and armies, and arms, and money, and provinces, and power—these things he reckoned as mere gossamer threads. But reckon up heavenly pleasures and then you will see his exceeding love for Christ.

The dignity of angels, or archangels, or anything else, meant less to him than the love of Christ. For he had within himself the greatest of all possessions—the love of Christ, and with it he considered himself the happiest of men. Without it he had no wish to belong to the company of dominations or principalities or powers. With this love he preferred to be numbered among the lowest of reprobates than without it to be on the heights among the most reputable. There was only one punishment in his eyes: to be without this love. This was hell to him, this was punishment, this was evil without end. Likewise the possession of the love of Christ was heaven: this was life, this was the whole world, this was being an angel, this was present joy, this was future joy, this was being a king, this was the Promise, this was goodness without end.

Apart from these he considered nothing else as pleasurable or painful. The whole visible world he despised as a piece of rotting foliage. Tyrants, in his eyes, and people breathing fire were just like gnats. Death, abuse, and punishment were children's playthings, as long as he was enduring them on account of Christ. Then he embraced them gladly, and he prized the embellishment of his chains more highly than if they were Nero's precious crown. Prison he occupied as if it were very heaven, and lashes and stripes he endured with more eagerness than other men hunt after prizes, prompting him to call pains a grace. Let me explain what I mean.

It would certainly be a prize *to depart and to be with Christ* (cf. Phil. 1:23). To stay on in the flesh was a trial. Nonetheless he chose the trial instead of the prize, and said it was more necessary for him. To be anathema from Christ was certainly a trial and a pain, nay surpassing a trial and a pain. To be with Christ was the prize.

But for the sake of Christ, he preferred to be anathema than to be with Christ.

Perhaps someone will say that all these things were pleasant to him because of Christ. I will agree that what would be distressing to us was very pleasant to him. Why do I mention dangers and other causes of wretchedness? His constant distress prompted him to say: *Who is weak, and I am not weak? Who is made to stumble, and I am not inflamed?* (2 Cor. 11:29).

One might say that there is a certain pleasure inherent in distress. Many who grieve at the deaths of their children find consolation if they are left alone with their tears. If their weeping is interrupted they feel the pain more intensely. Paul likewise drew consolation from weeping by day and night. No one ever grieved for his own sufferings as this man grieved for the sufferings of others. How great must have been his concern for the salvation of the Jews when he prayed to be excluded from the glory of Heaven if only they were saved![1] Isn't it clear from this that their loss of salvation was more grievous to him than his own? If not, he would not have prayed as he did. He would prefer to be lost himself, and derived consolation from that thought. It was not just a passing thought, but rather a vehement desire, expressed in the exclamation: *I have (great) sad-*

ness and continuous sorrow in my heart (Rom.
9:2). What then, can be compared to Paul, daily
grieving for every inhabitant of the world, for
every race and city, and for every single individual? He is more resolute than iron or adamant.
What word will describe this soul of his, golden
or adamantine? It is more durable than adamant,
more precious than gold or diamonds. It is more
solid than adamant and worth more than gold. To
what, then, will one compare it? To nothing, for
it is incomparable. If gold were as durable as adamant or adamant as precious as gold, then we
would have some basis for comparison. But why
compare Paul's soul to adamant or gold? Conjure
up the whole world and even then you will see the
world unworthy of the soul of Paul. For if this is
said of those wandering in sheepskins and in
caves in a hole in the earth [2] how much more fit-
tingly it is said of him?

And if the world is unworthy of him, what is
worthy? The heavens, perhaps? Even this is
found not to measure up. For if he preferred the
love of the Lord to the heavens and its inhabitants, would not the Lord, whose goodness surpasses Paul's as much as ordinary goodness
surpasses wickedness, prefer him to many
heavens? For God's love is not just proportioned

to ours, but outstrips it in an indescribable manner.

Let us consider the honors Paul received. He was caught up into Paradise, into the third heaven, made to share in secret words that man may not repeat.[3] He deserved the honor for as he walked the earth he did everything as if he were in the company of angels. Under the trappings of a mortal body he was angelic in his purity, and despite his human frailty he strove to be as angelic as the powers above. His course through the world was like that of a creature on wings: and like an incorporeal creature he despised toils and dangers. He despised everything on earth as if he had already attained the heavens, and exercised perpetual vigilance as if he already lived with the angels in heaven. To be guardians over particular peoples has often been assigned to angels, but none of them ever kept such guard over their particular assignment as Paul kept over the entire earth.

Do not object that it was not Paul himself that did these things. I agree. But even if he did not accomplish these things by his own power, he should not on that account be excluded from the praises for the accomplishments, since he made himself worthy of the grace that he received.

Michael's assignment was the Jewish race,[4] but Paul's was the earth and sea, the habited and the uninhabited world. And I say this, not to run down the angels,—God forbid!—but to show that man can be in the same company as the angels and enjoy almost equal status.

Why were angels not commissioned to preach the Gospel? So that you might have no excuse for slothfulness, or might not resort to a difference of nature in your sleep. Also that the net result might be greater. For surely it is marvelous and unexpected that a word springing from a tongue of clay should rout death, forgive sins, restore sight to the blind, and turn earth into heaven. This makes me marvel at the power of God; this makes me admire the zeal of Paul in receiving such grace and in preparing his soul for its reception.

I exhort you not merely to admire but to emulate this archetype of virtue. That way we will be able to share his crown. If it comes as a surprise to anyone to hear that we can match Paul in achievement if we imitate his example, let him listen to himself saying the same thing: *I have fought the good fight, I have finished the course, I have kept the faith. For the rest there is laid up for me a crown of justice which the Lord, the just Judge, will give to me in that day, yet not to me only but also to those who love His coming* (2 Tim. 4:7, 8). You see how he calls all to share in his achievement. Since then the same reward is open to all, let us all be zealous to prove worthy of the blessings that are promised. We should look not just to the greatness and glory of the life of virtue but also to the steadfastness of purpose through which this grace is attained, and to the fact that Paul was in no way different from ourselves. He was the same as we are and this should make what is very difficult appear light and easy to us, so that after this short period of labor we will continue to wear this lasting and immortal crown, through the grace and goodness of our Lord, Jesus Christ, to whom be glory and power now and always, forever and ever. Amen.

CHARITY WAS PAUL'S CROWNING VIRTUE

Gentle toward all, his ambition was to lead every man
to God—Concerned for temporal as well as spiritual
welfare of all—We should imitate Paul's charity, the
secret of his great sanctity.

The blessed Paul, manifesting the power of human zeal to enable us to fly to Heaven without the help of angels, archangels, and the other heavenly powers, at one time bids us imitate Christ through his example saying: *Be imitators of me as I am of Christ* (1 Cor. 11:1), and at another time omits mention of himself and leads us directly to God Himself saying: *Be you, therefore, imitators of God as very dear children* (Eph. 5:1). Then, to show that nothing is so conducive to this imitation as to think of others and of the common good, he adds: *Walk in charity* (Eph. 5:2). In the first quotation also, (*Be ye imitators of me*), he goes on immediately to talk of charity, showing that this virtue especially makes man God-like.

Notice how many other virtues there are inferior to this, which are man-centered—the fight with concupiscence, the war on gluttony, the campaign against avarice, the battle against anger. Charity, on the other hand, is something man shares with God. That is why Christ said: *Pray for those who calumniate you, so that you may be like your Father in heaven* (Mt. 5:44, 45).

Paul knew that charity was the crowning virtue and wished to cultivate it with the greatest care. No one ever so loved his enemies, no one ever did such good to those hostile to him, no one ever suffered so much for those that afflicted him.

He did not look to the sufferings they inflicted on him, but only remembered the human nature that they had in common, and the more savage they became the more he pitied their madness. A father whose son is crazy, pities him and weeps for him all the more as his madness and violence increase. Likewise with Paul. He diagnosed the morbidity that inspired those vehement attacks against himself and increased his concern for them accordingly. Hear, then, with what gentleness and sympathy he speaks to us about those who had scourged him [1] five times, stoned him, bound him, thirsted for his blood, and desired daily to tear him asunder: *For I bear them witness that they have zeal for God, but not according to knowledge* (Rom. 10:2). And again, restraining those who were hostile to them, he said: *Be not high-minded, but fear. For if God has not spared the natural branches, perhaps he may not spare thee either* (Rom. 11:20, 21). And when he saw the divine judgment coming upon them, he did the one thing that lay within his power—he wept and grieved for them continuously.

He often wept and grieved for them. He opposed those who wished to oppress them and strove to find even a shadow of an excuse for them. And when he failed to persuade them by his words because of their unbending stubbornness, he turned to continual prayers saying: *Brethren, my heart's desire and my prayer for you to God is in their behalf unto their salvation* (Rom. 10:1). He extended hope of better things to them, saying: *God does not change His mind about those to whom He gives His blessings or sends His call* (Rom. 11:29), so that they might not give up hope and die. All of which was proof of one who looked to their welfare and was exceedingly concerned about them, as when he said that: *There will come out of Sion the deliverer who will turn away impiety from Jacob* (Isa. 59:20, quoted in Rom. 11:26).

The sight of their destructiveness was a source of great remorse and pain to him, so he has constant recourse to palliatives for his sorrow, saying at one time: *There will come out of Sion a deliverer and he will turn away impiety from Jacob* (Rom. 11:26), and at another: *So they too have been disobedient that they too may experience the same mercy as you* (Rom. 11:31). Jeremias does the same thing, forcing himself to find extenuating circumstances for sinners, saying at one time: *Though our sins bear witness against us, act for Thy name's sake* (Jer. 14:7); and again: *Man's way is not his own: it is not in his power to control his steps* (Jer. 10:23), and again: *Remember that we are but dust* (Ps. 102:14).

It is customary for those pleading for sinners, if they have nothing good to say in their favor, to think up some shadow of an excuse for them which, even if it is not literally or theologically true, is calculated to console those who are grieving for their waywardness. Do not, then, examine the words too literally, but bear in mind that they are the words of a soul in distress, trying to make a case for sinners and judge them accordingly.

Do you think that was his attitude merely to his enemies and that he was not similarly disposed to outsiders? He was the gentlest of men both toward his own household and toward outsiders. Listen to his words to Timothy: *But the servant of the Lord must not quarrel, but be gentle towards all, ready to teach, patient, gently admonishing those who resist, in case God should give them repentance to know the truth, and they recover themselves from the snare of the devil, at whose pleasure they are held captive* (2 Tim. 2:24-26). Would you like to see how gentle he is to sinners? Listen to what he said to the Corinthians: *For I fear lest perhaps when I come I may not find you as I should wish* (2 Cor. 12:20), and a little later: *Lest when I come again God should humiliate me before you, and I should mourn over many who sinned before and have not re-*

*pented of the immorality and licentiousness that
they practised* (2 Cor. 12:21). And writing to the
Galatians he said: *My dear children, with whom
I am in labor again until Christ is formed in you*
(Gal. 4:19). Like a man weeping for his own sins
he wept for the man who had committed fornica-
tion and reassured him saying: *Assure him of
your love for him* (2 Cor. 2:8). Even when he
excommunicated him he did it in sorrow and
tears: *For I write to you in much affliction and
anguish of heart, not that you might be grieved
but that you might know the great love I have for
you* (2 Cor. 2:4). And again: *And I have become
to the Jews a Jew, to those under the Law as one
under the Law; to the weak I have become weak;
I became all things to all men that I might save
all* (1 Cor. 9:20-22). And again in another place:
*That I may present every man perfect in Christ
Jesus* (Col. 1:28).

You have seen a man, then, traversing the
entire earth. For it was his ambition to lead every
man to God and as far as lay within his power he
realized his ambition. As if the entire population
of the world were his children he was always in
a hurry, always on the go, always anxious to lead
all men to the Kingdom of Heaven, tending, exhorting, promising, praying, supplicating, fright-
ening away the demons, driving out those bent on

destruction, using personal appearances, epistles, words, deeds, disciples, raising up the fallen by his own efforts, giving a prop to those struggling on their feet, helping up those lying on the ground, ministering to the repentant, soothing the recalcitrant, threatening the hostile, and eyeing sternly the antagonistic. Like a general or a good doctor he joined in the fray and gave a helping hand, fending, defending, ministering, becoming all things to those engaged in the conflict.

He displayed great concern for their temporal as well as their spiritual affairs. Hear how he pleaded with the whole people on behalf of just one woman: *But I commend to you Phoebe, our sister, who is in the ministry at Cenchrae, that you may receive her, in the Lord as becomes saints and that you may assist her in whatever business she may have need of you* (Rom. 16:1). And again: *You know that the household of Stephanas are subject so that you also may be subject* (1 Cor. 16:15, 16). And again: *To such as these give recognition* (1 Cor. 16:18).

It is characteristic of the charity of the saints to give help even in temporal matters. Thus Eliseus gave temporal as well as spiritual assistance to the woman [2] that gave him hospitality. This prompted him to say: *Would you be commended*

to the King or the commander of the army?
(2 Kings 4:13).

And why do you wonder if Paul, when he calls some to himself, does not think it beneath his consideration to be concerned for their temporal welfare and makes reference to this in an epistle? Writing to Titus he says: *Help Zenas the lawyer and Apollos on their way, taking care that nothing be wanting to them* (Tit. 3:13). If he displayed such concern in his epistles he redoubled his efforts whenever he saw people in danger. Notice his regard for Onesimus [3] when he was writing to Philemon, and with what insistence and concern he writes. Consider how much Paul would do for others if he would not hesitate to compose an entire epistle for a slave, a fugitive who had stolen much of his master's belongings.

Only one thing he considered shameful: to overlook anything that contributed to salvation. Therefore he left no stone unmoved, he shrunk from no expenditure for those to be saved—words, deeds, his very life. He who submitted himself to countless deaths would not hesitate to spend any money if he had it. Why do I say 'if he had it,' when I can prove that he was unsparing of money even when he did not have it? Don't think that I am speaking in a paradox, but listen again to his own words: *I will most gladly spend and be spent myself for your souls* (2 Cor. 12:15). And addressing the Ephesians he said: *You yourselves know that these hands of mine have provided for my needs and those of my companions* (Acts 20:34).

In his greatness he was more ardent than any flame of fire in the crown of all virtues, namely, charity. Just as iron thrust into fire becomes all fiery, so Paul was consumed with charity and became charity incarnate. As if he were the common father of the whole world, he emulated the love of earthly fathers, or rather, he surpassed them in physical and spiritual love and concern and expended his money, his words, his body and soul, his all, for those he loved.

Therefore he calls charity the fulfillment of the law, [4] the bond of perfection, [5] the mother of all blessings, [6] and the beginning and end of virtue; [7] *Now the purpose of this charge is charity from a pure heart and a good conscience* (1 Tim. 1:5). And again: *For "Thou shalt not commit adultery; Thou shalt not kill"; and if there is any other commandment, it is summed up in this saying, "Thou shalt love thy neighbor as thyself"* (Rom. 13:9). Since, then, charity is the beginning and the end, and the sum of blessings, let us imitate Paul in this respect. For charity was the secret of his sanctity.

Do not count up the dead whom he resurrected, or the lepers whom he cleansed; God does not require such deeds from you. Just acquire Paul's charity and you will acquire the crown of perfection. Who said so? The cultivator of charity himself, the one who proposed it with signs and wonders, and other countless blessings. Because he so perfectly fulfilled the role of charity he knew its power to the full. It made him what he was; nothing so contributed to his goodness as this powerful virtue. Accordingly he said: *Strive after the greater gifts. And I point out to you a yet more excellent way* (1 Cor. 12:31), meaning charity, the finest and easiest road. Let us keep to that road, so that we may see Paul, or rather the Master of Paul, and gain incorruptible crowns, by the grace and loving kindness of our Lord Jesus Christ, to Whom be glory and power now and always, for ever and ever. Amen.

SERMON IV

ST. PAUL—A LIGHT TO THE WORLD—

His blindness coincided with God's call, which he answered freely. Many refused God's call in the Old and New Testament and in the recent past—Christianity has surmounted all obstacles because of the divine power of the Crucified. Paul helped its spread in spite of his own limitations and the poverty of his hearers—the unique power of the Gospel— Paul's part in diffusing its light.

51

The blessed Paul, in whose honor we are assembled today, was a light to the entire world. Yet at the time of his call by God he lost the light of his eyes. [1] This blindness gave light to the world. God in His mercy deprived him of sight because of his previous shortsightedness, in order to improve his subsequent vision.

In doing so He gave him at one and the same time a proof of His power and a foretaste of the sufferings that awaited him. He prefigured for him his life of preaching, indicating that he should turn his back on his former ways and follow Him blindly. Teaching him this He exclaimed: *If any one of you thinks himself wise let him become a fool that he may come to be wise* (1 Cor. 3:18). His sight could not improve unless he was first blinded. This made him turn his back on his former ways of thought which were a source of disturbance to him, and converted him completely to the Faith.

Let no one think, however, on hearing this, that the call he received brought pressure to bear upon him. He was free to go back again to where he came from. Many people, after witnessing other and greater wonders, went back again, both in the New and the Old Testaments, for instance Judas, Nabuchodonozor, Elymas the soothsayer, Simon, Ananias and Sapphira, and the entire Jewish people. But not Paul. Illuminated by the pure light he pursued his course and made his way to the heavens.

If you inquire after the cause of his blindness, listen to his words: *For you have heard of my former manner of life in Judaism, how beyond all measure I persecuted the Church, and ravaged it. And I advanced in Judaism above many of my contemporaries in my nation, showing much more zeal for the traditions of my fathers* (Gal. 1:13-14). Because of his restive zeal and fervor he needed an even greater restraint lest he should be carried forward by the force of his zeal and forget what had been said to him. Accordingly God first checked his frenzied zeal and used blindness as a means of restoring calm to the headlong words of his anger. Then he spoke to him and showed him the extent of His wisdom and the excess of His knowledge and that he might understand whom he was warring on, whom he could not endure when chiding or even when conferring benefits. For it was not darkness that blinded him, but excess of light that overshadowed him.

And why, you ask, did this not happen sooner? Do not inquire into this, or betray your curiosity but submit to the incomprehensible Providence of God which acts at the opportune moment. Paul acknowledges this, saying: *But when*

*it pleased Him who from my mother's womb set
me apart and called me by His grace to reveal
His Son in me* (Gal. 1:15, 16). Do not, then, betray excessive curiosity when Paul says this. Curiosity only proves rewarding when scandals are
removed. Let us learn, then, from him that no one
before his time, or he either, left to himself, dis-
covered Christ, which is why He said: *You have
not chosen me but I have chosen you* (Jn. 15:16).
But why, you ask did he not believe when he saw
the dead raised in His name? Did it profit him
nothing to see the lame walk, the devils put to
flight, the paralytics restored to health? For his
curiosity about the apostles did not allow these
marvels to escape his attention. He was standing
by when Stephen was being stoned and saw his
face radiant as an angel's but it did not do him
any good. Why? Because he had not yet received
the call.

Do not conclude from hearing this that the
call was mandatory. God does not compel. He
leaves men masters of their own will even after
He calls them. He revealed Himself to the Chosen
People when the occasion demanded but they rejected His call because of the honor they received
from men.

If any infidel interrupts at this point to ask
how we know Paul received a call from Heaven

which he answered, and 'why was I not called also', we will answer him as follows. Tell me, my good man, do you believe he was called? If you do, that should be sign enough for you. If you do not believe that he received a heavenly call why say: 'Why was I not called also?' If you believe, however, that he was called, that is sufficient sign for you. Believe, then, for God calls you also from Heaven if your soul is well disposed. If you are hostile and prejudiced, however, not even a call from Heaven will suffice for your salvation.

How often did the Chosen People hear a voice from Heaven and did not believe? How many signs did they witness in the Old Testament and the New and they became no better? In the Old dispensation they worshipped a calf [2] after witnessing countless wonders. But the harlot of Jericho [3] without seeing any such wonders showed wonderful faith in the spies. In the land of Promise the Chosen People saw signs and remained as obdurate as stones, but the Ninivites believed as soon as they saw Jonah, [4] and were converted and averted the Divine anger. In the New Testament the mere presence of Christ crucified turned the thief to adoration, but the Chosen People saw Him raising the dead to life yet they bound and crucified Him.

What of our own times? Did not the flame leaping from the foundations of the temple at

Jerusalem burn up those who were attempting to restore it and cause the survivors to cease from impious enterprise without converting them, however, or making them abandon their blind ways?

How great, too, were subsequent wonders and yet they were of no avail. The temple of Apollo, for instance, was struck by lightning and fell. The ruling Emperor was compelled to move the martyr's [5] body lying close by the oracle of Apollo, saying that he could not utter prophecy whilst the casket of Babylas lay in the vicinity. Later, the Emperor's uncle committed sacrilege on the sacred vessels and his body was eaten to death by worms. The steward of the imperial treasure, because of some offense he committed against the Church, was eviscerated and died. Again, the local fountains which normally overflowed dried up and rivers receded. This was unprecedented, except when the Emperor desecrated the place with his sacrifices and libations.

Why speak of the famine that swept the earth in the reign of the impious Emperor, [6] of his death in Persia, of his wandering before his death, his abandonment of his army in the midst of the enemy and their unexpected and miraculous return in spite of being trapped? When the impious emperor met with this wretched end a more god-fearing man [7] succeeded and immediately all trou-

bles ended. The army which had been ensnared
by the enemy and abandoned for lost, now re-
turned to safety at the divine behest. Are not such
events calculated to draw us to sanctity?

Isn't the present even more full of wonders?
Isn't the Cross preached and doesn't the whole
world rally to accept it? Isn't death proclaimed
unimportant, and all men are converted? Are not
countless men crucified: two thieves hung on
crosses on either side of Christ. Don't we have
many wise men? Many powerful men? Whose
name ever enjoyed such prestige? And why do I
speak just of the wise and powerful? There were
many great kings in the past. Which of them ever
won the allegiance of the whole world in such a
short span?

Do not make an issue of the various heretics
of different hue and color. They all proclaim
Christ even if they lack something in orthodoxy.
They all reverence the One who was crucified
under Pontius Pilate in Palestine.

Have not all these manifestations more pro-
bative force than any voice borne from Above?
Why has no king enjoyed as much sway as this
King in the face of so much opposition? For kings
have warred on Christianity, tyrants have opposed
it, whole peoples have risen against it, but, far

from being vanquished, we have persevered in ever-increasing splendor.

What, tell me, was the source of such power? Christ was a magician perhaps? Was He, then, the only magician to enjoy such power? Doubtless you have heard of the numerous magicians that still flourished in Persia and India. The name of none of them ever attained any prominence. That fraudulent soothsayer from Tyana [8] admittedly gained some notoriety. But where and when? In a remote area and for a short time, and then he was quickly snuffed out and disappeared, leaving behind no church, no following, nothing of that sort.

Why speak of departed magicians and sooth-sayers? Why have all the temples of the pagan gods ceased to function, those of Dodona and Claros, and all those workshops of profanity which are silent and shut down? Why do the devils tremble not only at the crucified but even at the bones of the martyrs? Why do they turn and disappear at the mere mention of the cross, which should rather make them laugh? Was it that the cross was noble and distinguished? On the contrary, it was an object of shame and reproach. Death on the cross was a criminal punishment, the most shameful of deaths, accursed by the Jews and abominated by the gentiles. How, then, could it

inspire fear in the devils? Was it not because of
the power of the One crucified? For if crucifixion
itself inspired terror it would be completely unworthy of the gods. Many others were crucified
before Christ and after Him, two were crucified
with Him. Would the devil take to flight if someone were to invoke the name of the crucified thief
or of some other crucified individual? Of course
not. He would only laugh. They would fly, however, as from fire, if the name of Jesus of Nazareth
is invoked.

What, then, do you say? What is the source
of His power? He was subversive perhaps? His
precepts were not those of a subversive, and there
were many such. He was a magician, perhaps?
That is not the import of His doctrines. Besides,
there has never been any scarcity of magicians.
He was a wise man, perhaps? Wise men have always been plentiful.

What, then, was the source of His power?
For no one even remotely approximated it. Obviously it was not because He was a magician,
or a subversive, but because He was a reformer
and possessed divine and invincible power. That
was the cause of His superiority and the reason
why He could inspire this tent-maker with the
power that his deeds attest.

For Paul was an ordinary man in the street, a tent-maker by trade, yet he was powerful enough to convert the Romans, Persians, Indians, Scythians, Ethiopians, Sauromati, Parthians, Medes, Saracens, I might say the whole world, in less than thirty years.

Tell me, how could a rustic, a tradesman in his workshop, scalpel in hand, acquire such philosophy, and teach it to others—peoples, cities, places —without possessing any gift of eloquence, without schooling or any professional training? Listen to his own unblushing words: *Even though I be rude in speech yet I am not so in knowledge* (2 Cor. 11:6). He also tells us that he had no money: *To this very hour we hunger and thirst, and are naked and buffeted* (1 Cor. 4:11). And why do I mention money when he often had not enough food to eat or clothes to wear? His disciple shows that he had not even any special distinction in trade, saying: *And, as he was of the same trade he stayed with Aquila and Priscilla, for they were tent-makers by trade* (Acts 18:3). His family was not distinguished. How could it be with such a means of livelihood? Neither was his country or his race. Yet when he came forward his mere appearance threw them into confusion and, like fire in straw or grass, exhausted the devil's resources and converted everything to his own way of thinking.

The fact that he attained such eminence in spite of his limitations is not the only remarkable feature. Most of his disciples were also poor, unskilled, without formal education, living in hunger, undistinguished sons of undistinguished parents. He testifies to this himself and is not ashamed to mention their poverty, or rather to plead for their necessities of life: *I will set out,* he says, *for Jerusalem to minister to the saints* (Rom. 15:25). And again: *On the first day of the week let each one of you put aside and lay up at home so that collections may not have to be made after I have come* (1 Cor. 16:2). Because most of his disciples were from the ranks of the unsophisticated, he said in his letter to the Corinthians: *Consider your own call, that there were not many wise according to the flesh, not many mighty, not many noble* (1 Cor. 1:26), and in fact they were not merely not of noble birth but actually of very poor origin: *The weak things of this world has God chosen and the things that are not to bring to naught the things that are* (1 Cor. 1:27, 28).

Perhaps they were unsophisticated and unlettered, you suggest, but were skilled in persuasive speech? No, not even this, as Paul shows also: *And I came to you not with pretentious speech or wisdom, announcing unto you the witness of Christ. For I determined not to know anything among you, except Jesus Christ and him crucified. And my speech and my preaching were not in the persuasive words of wisdom* (1 Cor. 2: 1, 2, 4). The Gospel he had to preach was sufficient to attract an audience. Listen to his words on this score: *For the Jews ask for signs and the Greeks look for "wisdom"; but we, for our part, preach a crucified Christ—to the Jews indeed a stumbling-block and to the Gentiles foolishness* (1 Cor. 1:22, 23).

But he enjoyed freedom from care, you say? On the contrary, he was in a constant atmosphere of danger: *And I was with you in weakness and in fear and in much trembling* (1 Cor. 2:3). His disciples were exposed to the same troubles as himself: *But call to mind the days gone by, in which, after you had been enlightened, you endured a great conflict of sufferings; partly by being made a public spectacle through reproaches and tribulations, and partly by working common cause with those who fared thus, for you have joyfully accepted the plundering of your own goods* (Heb. 10:32-34). And again, writing to the people of Thessalonica, he says: *You also have suffered the same things from your own countrymen as they have . . . They are displeasing to God, and are hostile to all men* (1 Thess. 2:14-15). And in his letter to the Corinthians he says: *For as the*

sufferings of Christ abound in us, so also as you
are partakers of the sufferings, so will you also be
of the comfort (cf. 2 Cor. 1:5, 7). And to the Galatians: *Have you suffered so much in vain, if in-*
deed it be vain (Gal. 3:4). The preacher, then,
was poor and undistinguished. His preaching had
nothing to recommend it, but was, in fact, a
stumbling-block. His hearers were poor, weak, and
of no importance. Dangers were constantly press-
ing and hovering over both teachers and taught.
The preaching was centered on One crucified.
How could it succeed? Is it not obvious that there
was some divine, ineffable power? Perfectly obvious, especially in the light of a contrast: When
you see the opposite qualities concurring in one
person—I mean wealth, nobility of birth, greatness
of country, rhetorical skill, security, and much attention to detail—what is the explanation if these
fresh faggots are spent and the opposite prevails?

It is the same as if an Emperor with armies,
arms, and a strong line-up, failed to conquer a bar-
baric hoard, while an ill-clad beggerman with no
weapon in his hand or coat on his back should enter the lists single-handed and accomplish what
those armed and equipped for the job failed to do.
Do not, then, remain prejudiced but make a daily
decision to hold the cross in veneration.

If you see on the one hand an Emperor marking out cities for conquest, throwing a siege line around them, bringing up his battering rams to the walls, forging weapons, enlisting soldiers, displaying endless resources, yet failing to take a single city, and on the other hand another man without uniform and bareheaded, succeeding in winning not one or two or twenty cities, but countless cities throughout the world, and winning over the inhabitants besides, you would hardly describe that as a work of mere human power.

The present situation is obviously similar. God consented to be crucified with thieves and allowed imposters to appear before the Incarnation for two reasons: that the startling contrast would proclaim the superiority of the truth even to the most uncomprehending, and that you might learn that He is not just one of them but differs from them totally. For nothing can shadow His glory, neither the fact that the thieves shared in His sufferings nor suffered at the same time. The pair of thieves reduced to silence those who would say that the devils feared the cross merely and not the power of the One crucified. If the temper of the times are invoked to explain everything He did, Theodas and Judas [9] can be produced as attempting to bolster false claims with many other signs and coming to a bad end. As I said God's

purpose in allowing them was to set forth the
truth in ever clearer light. That too is why He allowed pseudo prophets to appear in the time of
the prophets, and pseudo apostles in the time of
the apostles, that you might learn that nothing
can overshadow His deeds.

Let me give you another instance of the marvelous and remarkable power of the Gospel. I will
show you that it increases and prospers even while
it is under attack. Some proclaimed this Gospel at
Rome while Paul was being persecuted. Wishing
to increase Nero's hostility to Paul, they under-
took to preach the Gospel so that with its spread
and an increase in its following, the tyrant's anger
might be stimulated and his ferocity increased.
Paul tells the Philippians of this: *I wish you to
know, brethren, that my experiences have turned
out rather for the advancement of the gospel, so
that the greater number of the brethren gaining
courage from my chains, have dared to speak the
word of God more freely and without fear. Some
indeed preach Christ even out of envy and contentiousness, but some also out of good will. Some
out of contentiousness, not sincerely, thinking to
stir up affliction for me in my chains; some out of
love, knowing that I am appointed for the defense
of the gospel. But what of it? Provided only that
in every way, whether in pretence or in truth,*

Christ is being proclaimed (Phil. 1:12-18). You see how many preached through contention but nonetheless truth triumphed through its very enemies.

Together with such enmity there were other hostile factors. For the old laws were no help. Instead they were hostile and inimical, as were the malice and ignorance of slanderers. They failed to recognize a heavenly King, terrible and glorious, but thought of Christians introducing tyranny to earth, and wrestled with it individually and collectively, combining malice and ignorance in their slanderous charges.

They acted collectively as if Christians were a threat to the constitution and the rule of the law, and individually as if every single home were in danger of being undermined and destroyed. Father was at war with son and son turned against father, wives against husbands and husbands against wives, daughters against mothers, relations against relations, friends against friends.

It was a war of many facets and phases, creeping into homes, dividing relations, disrupting law and order, and disturbing the public peace. Ancestral customs were terminated, sacred festivities and the cult of the gods were brought low, all of which had been given priority by time-honored legislation.

Besides, the suspicion of tyranny caused them to be driven out everywhere. One could not say that all this was done by the Gentiles, and that the Chosen People held their peace, for they too intensified the opposition inasmuch as Christianity constituted a threat to their way of life. *"This man never ceases,"* they said, *"speaking words of blasphemy against the Holy Place and the Law"* (Acts 6:13).

Nonetheless, while the fire raged in every quarter—the home, the city, the country, the desert, the Gentiles, the leaders, rulers and ruled, relatives, earth, sea, the imperial family, with everyone arousing everybody else to ferocity and becoming more savage than wild beasts,—this blessed man leapt into the smouldering embers, stood in the midst of the wolves and, though pelted from every side, refused to capitulate but converted them all to the side of truth.

I could recall other battles of even greater ferocity, the battle waged by pseudo apostles which annoyed Paul more than any other, the weakness within his own ranks, for many believed them and perished. But eventually he was also a match for them. How and with what assistance? *For our weapons* he said, *are not carnal, but powerful before God to the demolishing of strongholds, the destroying of reasoning—yes, of every lofty thing that exalts itself against the knowledge of God* (2 Cor. 10:4-5).

Accordingly, everything was changed and rapidly transformed. Just as in a forest fire thorns are quickly consumed and yield to the force of the flames clearing the brushwood, so too everything yielded to the burning words of Paul—the cult of demons, festivals, panegyrics, ancestral customs, destructive laws, people's anger, the threats of tyrants, the plottings of domestics, the subversive activities of pseudo apostles.

Or rather, just as the rays of the rising sun put darkness to flight, and make the wild beasts seek shelter and rest, [10] causing thieves to take to their heels, murderers to seek refuge in caves, pirates to disappear, body snatchers to depart, and adulterers, thieves, and subversives to leave and seek a lengthy seclusion lest they be detected by the light of day, and everything becomes bright and luminous on earth and sea as the rays beam down from above on waters, mountains, villages and cities; so, too, in the clear light of the Gospel as it was disseminated by Paul, error was banished, truth introduced in its place, there was an end to the ashes and the smoke of sacrifices, cymbals and tympana clanged no more, the drunken revels, adulteries, and shameful practices associated with pagan rites in temples came to a

complete standstill. It was like the disappearance
of wax in a fire, or chaff eaten by the flames.

The flame of truth rose in splendor over the
ashes and towered to the heavens. Those who
tried to impede it contributed most to its rise and
spread. Exposure to danger could not cramp its
progress or growth. The tyranny of inveterate
habit and the deep-rootedness of ancestral law and
custom were equally ineffective; neither the diffi-
culties inherent in its doctrine nor anything else
could impede its diffusion.

To learn its real strength, present a challenge
to the Gentiles. I do not mean dangers, death, and
famine, but even a small loss of goods, and you will
see them quickly falter. Christ, on the other hand,
thrives on opposition, slaughter, and every kind
of hostility. And why speak of those worthless and
despicable Gentiles? Let us review those of them
that were celebrated and gained a reputation for
philosophy—Plato, Diagoras, Anaxagoras of Cla-
zomenae, and many others of that ilk, and you
will see the superiority of the Gospel. For after
Socrates took the poison, some departed to Megara
for fear of suffering the same fate. Others quit
fatherland and freedom and won only one female
convert to philosophy. The philosopher from
Citium[11] died and left us his ideal state depicted
in his writings. And yet there was nothing to im-

pede them—no danger, or lack of training, for they were skilled in speech, and wealthy, and belonged to a country held in high repute, yet they failed to achieve success.

Error is such that it is dissipated even without opposition, but truth prevails in the midst of hostile forces. Truth proclaims itself and is in no need of words, since the whole world lends it its voice—cities, fields, the earth, the sea, the inhabited and uninhabited world, the tops of the mountains. It has left no place bereft of its goodness, but has filled everywhere with the blessings that come from the heavens through the tongue of Paul, and the grace infused into him. Because he corresponded with the grace, the grace shone all the more luminously in him, and more than what we have spoken of was accomplished through his tongue.

Since God so honored our nature as to make one man the source of so many blessings, let us strive to resemble him, and refuse to think that this is impossible. I have often said, and I will continue to say, that he had the same body as we have, the same nourishment, the same soul, but he had great will-power and remarkable zeal. This made him what he was. Let no one be incredulous, or turn a deaf ear. If you prepare your mind, nothing can stop you from receiving the same grace. For God is not a respector of persons.[12] He made Paul, and He made you; He is your Lord as much as Paul's, and as He proclaimed Paul He wishes to crown you. Let us, therefore, consecrate and dedicate ourselves to God, that receiving the same abundant grace we may obtain the same blessings by the grace and mercy of our Lord Jesus Christ to whom be glory and power for ever and ever. Amen.

Sermon V

PAUL WAS MORTAL, POOR,
AND OF LOWLY BIRTH,
BUT BECAME GREAT AND
SHOWED US THE WAY TO GREATNESS

Sin is the one cause for sadness—Strength of will
allied to grace makes a man virtuous—Paul's will was
completely united to God's will—He became all things
to all men for the spread of the Gospel—Like a good
doctor he varies his treatment for different spiritual
maladies—Paul's modesty even in apparent boasting
about himself—His rebukes were equally tactful and
timely.

73

Where are those now who are in the habit of finding fault with death, saying that this suffering and corruptible body hinders them from attaining to virtue? Let them listen to the achievements of Paul and cease their wretched slanders. What injury has death inflicted on our race? What obstacle does a corruptible body offer to virtue? Consider Paul and you will see that mortality is in fact our greatest blessing.

For if Paul were not mortal he could not say, or rather, he could not show what he said through his deeds, that *I die daily, I affirm it, by the very pride that I take in you in Christ Jesus* (1 Cor. 15:31). We have only to be always keen-spirited and zealous and nothing can stop us from being in the foremost ranks. Was not Paul mortal? Was he not a man of lowly birth? Was he not poor? Had he not to earn his daily bread? Had he not a body subject to every natural need? What prevented him from becoming as great as he did? Absolutely nothing.

Let no one, then, lose heart because of poverty or lowly birth. Let no one be pained because he belongs to the lower classes. The only cause for sorrow is an emasculated soul and an enervated mind. The one obstacle to virtue is spiritual weakness and mental debility, nothing else. This is plain from this blessed man who brought us together on the present occasion. For just as none of those qualities was an obstacle to virtue in his case, so the opposite qualities were of no benefit to outsiders, things like skill in speech, abundance of wealth, nobility of birth, great reputation, or political standing.

But why speak of men? Or rather, how long will I confine my speech to the earth when I could speak of heavenly beings, principalities, powers, the cosmic governors of the darkness of this age? [1] Have not all these powers come to be judged by Paul and those like him? *Do you not know,* he says, *that we shall judge angels?* (1 Cor. 6:3).

Let sin, then be the one cause for grief and virtue, the one cause for gladness and joy. If we seek virtue there is nothing to prevent us from being like Paul. For grace was not the only cause of his greatness. There was also the strength of his own will. Or rather, grace was added to his strength of will. He had both kinds of qualities to perfection, what God infused into him and what he acquired by his own will. Would you like to hear his divine qualities? The devils feared contact with his garments. I don't wonder at this because Peter's shadow put diseases to flight. What I do marvel at is his activity before he got grace, from the very starting point and commencement of his career. Without this divine power, and before receiving ordination, he was so consumed with zeal for Christ that he stirred up a whole people against himself. When he saw himself in such dangers, with the city under siege, he was lowered down the wall in a basket. [2] This escape did not cause him dejection, or cowardice, or fear; instead it was a source of greater zeal and he submitted to dangers for the Gospel; he yielded to none in his zeal for preaching but took up his cross and followed.

With the recent example of Stephen staring him in the face, and his enemies mustered against him breathing murder, and anxious to consume him body and bones, Paul did not recklessly run into dangers, or relapse into timidity and flee. Life was very dear to him because of the opportunities for good which it afforded him. It was also very cheap to him, because of his transcendent philosophy and of his extreme desire to join Christ in Heaven. As I have always said about him, and always will say, no one was so ambivalent in his attitude, ever ready to take the side that offered most advantage. Thus, no one was so in love with life here below or with those who loved life most. At the other extreme, no one ever thought so little of life, even the ones who quit it with the greatest abandon.

He had so completely rid himself of every human desire that there was no attachment left to anything here below. His whole will was united to the will of God. So at one time he thought life on earth was more necessary than the company and conversation of Christ, at another time it seemed so burdensome and tiresome that it made him groan and long for the deliverance of death. His only wish was for what would prove profitable to him with Christ, even if the result was the opposite of what preceded.

He was a man of many parts and many facets. I do not mean that he was acting. God forbid! But he became all things to all men, whatever was demanded by the needs of the Gospel and the salvation of mankind. In this he imitated his Master.

For God Himself appeared as man when it was necessary to do so. In olden times He also manifested Himself in fire when it was necessary to do so. More recently, in the uniform of an armed soldier, or in the likeness of an old man, or in a breath of wind, or as a traveler, or as true man and as such He did not refuse to die.

I find it necessary to repeat, in saying 'when it was necessary to do so' that no one should think God *had* to do what I have mentioned, but merely that He did those things through His love for man.

At another time He sat on a throne, again on the Cherubim. He acted as He did in accordance with the particular requirements of the moment. Accordingly He said through the prophet: *I have multiplied visions and I have used similitudes by the ministry of the prophets* (Os. 12:10).

And so Paul, in imitation of his Master, should not be blamed, if at one time he acted as a Jew, at another as an outsider; at one time standing up for the Law, at another despising it; at one time embracing the present life, at another holding it in slight esteem; at one time demanding contributions, at another rejecting offerings; at one time offering sacrifices and shaving his head, at another pronouncing anathema on those who did so; at one time championing circumcision, at another repudiating it. What he did appeared to be contradictory but the intention and determination behind the deeds were logical and consistent.

His one and only object was the salvation of those that heard and saw him; accordingly at one time he praised the Law, at another he downgraded it. In his deeds and his words he may have been ambivalent and complex, but his mind and personality remained unchanged; he preserved his identity and adapted his words to the occasion. For this, he should be proclaimed and applauded.

A doctor's treatment varies: he cauterizes, prescribes diet, operates, administers drugs, forbids foods and drinks, leaves some wounds uncovered, covers others, prescribes a phial full of cool waters for fevers. He is not censured for not employing uniformity of treatment, or for constant change. Rather, you praise his art when you see the confidence with which he administers apparently conflicting and injurious remedies, and guarantees that they are safe. This is a man proficient in his craft.

If we accept a doctor who varies his treatment, we should be even more ready to proclaim Paul's psychology as he ministers to those who are ill. For the sick in soul need variety of treatment no less than the sick in body. To treat them in a uniform and stereotyped manner would jeopardize their salvation.

We can hardly wonder at men acting thus since the omnipotent God uses the same methods of treatment and does not rely on a single direct approach. He wishes us to be good of our own free will, not under constraint or duress, so He needs some variety of approach, not because of any lack of ability on His part—far from it—but because of our weakness. A mere nod from Him, or rather a mere act of will, can accomplish all His wishes. But we, once we have become masters

of ourselves, no longer submit to God in everything. If He then forced us against our will, He
would be taking away what He had given us. I
mean free will. To avoid doing so He needs a
variety of approaches.

These observations of mine are not made at
random, but to explain the complexity and wisdom of the blessed Paul. Consequently, when you
see him avoiding dangers you should admire him
just as much as when he meets them head on. The
one bespeaks wisdom, the other bravery. Boastfulness of speech should command the same
respect as moderation. The one bespeaks magna-
nimity, the other modesty. Praise him as much for
magnifying as for minimizing his deeds: the one is
the mark of a soul without guile, the other of a
soul full of love and kindness. The object of his
actions is to achieve the salvation of the multitude.
Consequently he said: *For if we were out of our
mind, it was for God; if we are sane, it is for you*
(2 Cor. 5:13).

No one else had such reason to be boastful,
yet no one was so free of arrogance. Consider
these words of his: *Knowledge puffs up* (1 Cor.
8:1), words that we all should make our own.
Yet he certainly was as knowledgeable as any man
ever born. Nonetheless this did not make him
arrogant but modest: *We know in part and we*

prophesy in part (1 Cor. 13:9), and *Brethren, I do not consider that I have laid hold of it already* (Phil. 3:13), and *If anyone thinks that he knows anything, he has not yet known anything* (1 Cor. 8:2).

Fasting, too, puffs up with pride, as the Pharisee showed when he said *I fast twice a week* (Lk. 18:12). But Paul, not only when enduring fasts, but even when starving, called himself *one born out of due time* (1 Cor. 15:8).

Why do I speak of wisdom and fasting? For though he was closer to God in his constant prayer than any of the prophets or apostles, he was on that account all the more humble.

Do not quote for me what you find in his letters, for he kept more to himself than he expressed. He did not tell everything, for that might make him look boastful. Neither did he keep silent about everything, for that would set the tongues of the pseudo apostles wagging against him. Nothing he did was haphazard: everything was ordered and well-planned. Manifold as his actions appear, they all merit the same universal praise. Let me expand on this.

It is a very good thing not to boast about oneself. Paul, however, did it so becomingly that he merits more praise for speaking than if he had kept silent. If he had kept silent he would be more deserving of censure than those who shamelessly sing their own praises. If he had not sung his own praises, everything would have been lost, and his enemies' stock would have soared. He knew how to avail of a favorable opportunity and with just the right tact to do what was apparently wrong, thereby gaining as much glory as for obeying the commandments.

Paul gained more glory by his boasting than another would gain for keeping silent about his good deeds, for no one gained as much by silence as Paul did by boasting.

The great wonder is, not that he spoke about himself, but that he spoke just the right amount. He did not just seize on the favorable moment and use it for over-indulging in self-praise; he knew when it was time to stop. This was not to please himself, and he called himself a fool so as to deter others from indulging in destructive self-praise just for the sake of praise, while he confined this practice to when the occasion demanded.

It was likely that others, looking to him, would follow his example thoughtlessly and without reason. This happens in the case of doctors. Often what one man prescribes with care is used carelessly by another and the effect of the prescription is blunted and thwarted. To avoid similar complications notice how Paul surrounds his practice with great circumspection, delaying self-praise not just once, or twice, but many times and saying: *Would to God that you could bear with a little of my foolishness* (2 Cor. 11:1-2) and again: *What I am saying, I am not speaking according to the Lord, but as it were in foolishness* (2 Cor. 11:17, 21). *In which* (i.e. in foolishness) *if anyone dares, I dare too.* And he did not regard this saying as adequate but in his reluctance to sound boastful he conceals his identity, saying: *I know a man,* and again: *of such a man I will boast; but of myself I will not boast.* After all this he adds: *I have become foolish! You have forced me* (2 Cor. 12:2, 5, 11).

When one sees this holy man's reluctance and hesitancy to boast about himself even when absolute necessity demanded it, constantly bridling his speech as if it were a horse rushing downhill despite his economy of words, who in the face of that would be so foolish and so utterly insensitive as to indulge in excessive self-adulation instead of confining such activity to the barest minimum dictated by necessity?

Would you like me to tell you of another trait of his? We should marvel at the fact that, not satisfied with the testimony of conscience, he also taught us how we should act in each of these circumstances. He excuses his self-praise on the grounds that necessity demanded it, but also takes the opportunity to teach others not to flee the occasion if it presents itself and not to seize it unseasonably.

The thread of his remarks is something like this: It is a great evil to indulge in big talk about oneself. Dearly beloved, it is a mark of extreme folly to deck out one's own praises, without any necessity or compelling reason. Such speech cannot be in accordance with the Lord, but is rather a mark of insanity, depriving us of all that we have gained by our sweat and toil. Such a warning he seemed to address to all, and especially when he displayed reluctance to speak even when necessity called for it.

There was also the remarkable fact that he did not pour out everything when the need presented itself, but managed to conceal the greater part of his achievements. *I will come,* he says, *to visions and revelations of the Lord. I forbear, lest any man should reckon me beyond what he sees in me or hears from me* (2 Cor. 12:1, 6). These words are a lesson to all of us not to reveal everything about ourselves, even when we have to speak, but only such things as will benefit our audience.

So too with Samuel. There is nothing untoward in mentioning this holy man, for praises of him are for our benefit. He too indulged in self-praise on occasion, and spoke of his own good works. But in what way? He only spoke such things as would benefit his audience. He did not dilate on temperance, or humility, or forgiveness of injuries, but on what? On that which a king of that time most needed to know—on justice, and on remaining immune to bribery.

David, too, indulges in self-praise only to the extent that it can benefit his audience. He did not specify any virtue, but merely led a bear and a lion[3] into view, nothing more. To speak more than is necessary is a mark of ambition and boastfulness: to stick to what the present demands as necessary and useful is the work of a friend keeping the needs of his friends in view.

That is what Paul did. He was slandered and charged with not being an approved apostle, and having genuine power. Necessity demanded that he should produce evidence that would clearly show his worth. Notice how it was not praise for the sake of praise, but to enlighten his audience:

Firstly, he showed that he acted out of necessity;

Secondly, he called himself a fool, and used many terms of self-reproach;

Thirdly, he did not tell everything, but concealed the greater part;

Fourthly, he concealed his identity and said,
"I know a man. . . ;"

Fifthly, he did not produce all his virtues as
evidence, but only those which the occasion called for.

He preserved this balance both in praise of
himself and in apparent dispraise of others. To
rebuke a brother is among the things forbidden.
Yet Paul's rebukes were so timely that they were
more laudable than praises. For instance, once or
twice he called the Galatians foolish (Gal. 3:1),
and the Cretans *lazy gluttons* and *evil beasts*
(Tit. 1:12), and makes this a text for his preaching.

By his example he established definitions and
a norm that in handling those hostile to God we
should not use gentleness but should resort to
words that hit home. Indeed he laid down norms
for everything: his every word and deed is ac-
ceptable, whether rebuking or praising, hard
words or soft, self-praising or self-effacing, boasting or deprecating. Why wonder if rebuke and
abuse are praiseworthy, seeing that slaughter,
deceit, and guile found favor in the Old Testament and the New? Carefully examining all these
things, let us marvel at Paul and give glory to
God and so imitate him that we may obtain everlasting blessings by the grace and goodness of our
Lord, Jesus Christ to Whom be glory and power,
now and always, forever and ever. Amen.

Sermon VI

THE ANSWER TO CRITICS OF PAUL:

His apparent human weaknesses (e.g. fear of suffering)
only add to the greatness of his spiritual achievement—
Strength of will triumphed over weakness of nature—
His occasional display of anger was justified—
His apparent estrangement from John Mark was in the
interests of preaching which is the most onerous of tasks.

89

Today, dearly beloved, it is your wish that we deal with those aspects of Paul's wonderfully active life which afford a handle for criticism to some. We will see that these activities no less than his others contribute rather to his greatness and renown.

What is it that is considered worthy of criticism? His fear of blows, you say, was conspicuous. It was obvious when he was beaten with rods, and not only then, but also at the house of the dealer in purple [1] when he gave trouble to those who wanted to help him escape from prison. His only concern in all these incidents was to provide for his own safety and not to fall back again into the same predicaments.

What are we to say to such charges? Only this, that nothing shows his greatness and might more than these charges. Why? Because, when the occasion demanded, he displayed the fortitude of an incorporeal angel in facing what appeared to be such formidable threats in spite of such natural deficiencies as a soul that was neither dare-devil nor desperate and a body that recoiled from blows and trembled before the lash.

When you see him, then, cowering and fearful, remember those words with which he mounted to the skies and vied with angels, saying: *Who shall separate us from the love of Christ? Shall tribulation, or distress, or persecution, or hunger, or danger, or the sword?* (Rom. 8:35).

Recall those words in which he reckoned these things as naught, saying: *For our present light affliction, which is for the moment, prepares for us an eternal weight of glory that is beyond all measure; while we look not at the things that are seen, but at the things that are not seen* (2 Cor. 4:17-18). Add to this the daily tribulations, the daily dying. And let the reckoning restore both admiration for Paul and self-confidence in yourself.

His apparent weakness of nature is the clearest proof of his virtue, the fact that he achieved such strength without losing anything of the weakness proper to the rest of men.

The enormity of the dangers he had to face, many felt, provided this handle for criticism and prompted them to suspect that his greatness came from superhuman power. Accordingly he was allowed to suffer so that you might learn that his nature was the same as everybody else's, but that his will power made him not just a superman but one of the angels. With such a soul and such a body he endured a thousand deaths, making light of things present and to come. This prompted these marvelous words which many find incredible: *For I could wish to be anathema myself from Christ for the sake of my brethren, who are my kinsmen according to the flesh* (Rom. 9:3).

It is possible, if only we have the will, to overcome every weakness of nature by strength of will, and none of the commandments of Christ are impossible to man. If we utilize such strength as we have, God will greatly assist us and will render us immune from all the dangers that beset us.

To fear blows is not reprehensible; what is reprehensible is to commit sin through fear of blows. The one that fears but remains unscarred in the contest is more to be admired than the one who does not fear. For this brings his will power more into evidence. To fear blows is natural; but to refuse to sin on account of this fear is a triumph of will over weak human nature. To grieve is not reprehensible, but to do or say something displeasing to God on account of grief is.

If I were to say that Paul was not human, you could rightly raise objections about human frailties, in order to disprove my statement. But if I say and affirm that he was human, and no better than us by nature but superior in will power only, your objections would be pointless, or rather they would be to Paul's credit, in that they would show how he triumphed over nature in spite of such natural frailties. As well as praising him, you also seal the lips of those who malign him, taking away from them the excuse of human frailty, and compelling them to exercise will power.

But, you object, he sometimes feared death. Now that is also perfectly natural. *For we who are in this tent sigh under our burden* (2 Cor. 5:4). And again: *we ourselves groan within ourselves* (Rom. 8:23). You see how he counterbalanced weakness of nature with strength of will. Many martyrs, on their way to death, have often grown pale and been filled with fear and trembling. But that is what made them remarkable: the fact that though they feared death they went forward to meet it for the sake of Jesus. Likewise Paul, though he feared death did not avoid Gehenna because of his love for Christ; though he trembled before death he longed to be dissolved.

And it was not only he, but the head of the apostles also often said that he was ready to lay down his life though he had a dread of death. [2] Listen to what Christ has to say to him on that score: *But when thou art old they will lead thee where thou wouldst not* (Jn. 21:18), meaning a weakness of nature, not of will.

Nature manifests its own weaknesses in spite of us and we cannot eliminate such weaknesses however ardently we wish or try. We cannot be blamed for such weaknesses; instead, they elicit praise. How could fear of death be reprehensible?

Is it not rather praiseworthy to refrain from doing anything sinful out of fear? There is nothing blameworthy in having a nature that is weak, but only in giving into those weaknesses. That man is rightly regarded as great and admirable who overcomes weakness of nature by strength of will. In this he shows how effective strength of will is, and he shuts up those critics who say: Why were we not made good by nature? For what difference would it be to be by nature what we can be through free will? In fact it is far better to be good voluntarily than naturally, in that it brings greater rewards and more distinguished praise.

What if nature is strong? It can gain in strength if you wish to maintain your strength of will. Don't you see that the martyrs' bodies were hacked by swords, that their bodies yielded to the steel, but their wills refused to be vanquished.

Tell me, did you not see in Abraham's case, the will triumphing over the flesh, [3] when he was ordered to sacrifice his son? His will was clearly stronger than his natural inclination. Did you not see the same thing happen in the case of the Three Youths? [4] Haven't you heard the secular proverb that the will by habit becomes second nature? I would even say 'first' nature, as I have proved by my preceding remarks.

You see that nature can become strong and firm, if the will is well-trained and vigilant, and that goodness resulting from free will gains more plaudits than if we were born good. Goodness freely acquired is the only real goodness. I especially applaud him when he says; *I chastise my body and bring it into subjection* (1 Cor. 9:27), when I realize that to be virtuous he had to work at it, and in this he removes an argument for lethargy from his followers who might think that his virtue was easily come by. Again when he says: *I am crucified to the world* (Gal. 6:14), I applaud his will power. Innate strength can be reproduced by strength of will. If we introduce into view that paragon of virtue itself we will find that he strove to strengthen his natural powers with whatever strength of will he possessed.

He grieved when he was beaten, but he made light of the blows as the angelic powers who have no feeling; this you can see from his own words, which can be applied also to our nature. When he says: *The world is crucified to me, and I to the world* (ibid.), and again: *It is now no longer I that live, but Christ lives in me* (Gal. 2:20), what else does he say except that he had quit the body as also when he says: *There was given a thorn for the flesh, a messenger of Satan*

(2 Cor. 12:7), this only goes to show that pain only reaches the body.

Not that it does not penetrate inward but that it is excluded and repelled by superior strength of will. When he utters all those other marvelous statements, such as that he rejoices in being whipped and glories in being chained, what else does he mean except what I have just been saying. When he says: *I chastise my body and bring it into subjection lest perhaps after preaching to others I myself should be rejected* (1 Cor. 9:27), he is talking about weakness of nature achieving nobility of will in the manner I have explained.

The two sides are stressed in this way lest you might think that the greatness of his achievements belonged to a superhuman nature, causing you to despair; or, on the other hand, lest the smallness might make you depreciate his sanctity, and this in turn would make you turn from despair to presumption about salvation. Therefore he also stresses the grace of God, seeming to over emphasize it, but really gratefully acknowledging it, lest you think that it was solely through his own efforts.

He also mentions his own part, so that you will not leave everything to God and just sit there sleeping and belching.

You will find canons and norms for everything, laid down by him with exactitude.

He also cursed on occasion, for instance, Alexander, the coppersmith (2 Tim. 4:14). What of that? His words were said more in sorrow than in anger, and in the interests of truth. It was not his own feelings that were hurt, but he felt that he resisted his teaching. *He has vehemently opposed*, he says, not 'me' but *our words* (2 Tim. 4:15). So his curse is both an expression of his love for the truth and of concern for his disciples. For clearly they were all scandalized at the adversaries of truth escaping unharmed, and that prompted his words.

He also prayed against others, saying: *Indeed it is just on the part of God to repay with affliction those who afflict us* (2 Thess. 1:6), not in any desire that they pay the penalty—heaven forbid—but to bring prompt consolation to those in distress. Therefore he adds: *to give the afflicted rest* (ibid. v. 7). When he suffered any distress, notice how he philosophizes about it, and returns good for evil saying: *We are reviled and we bless, we are persecuted and we bear with it, we are maligned and we entreat* (1 Cor. 4:13). If you say that what was said or done for others was prompted by anger, then presumably Elymas, the sorcerer, was blinded and abused in anger (Acts 13:11), and Ananias and Sapphira were put to death by Peter in anger (Acts 5:4, 5). No one is such a fool or a half-wit as to make such an allegation.

We will find Paul saying and doing many other things which seem high-handed, yet it is especially these that show his moderation. When he handed the Corinthian adulterer to Satan, he did it with great love and affectionate disposition, and he shows this in his second Epistle. And when he threatens his enemies in the words: *the wrath of God has come upon them to the utmost* (1 Thess. 2:16), his words are not full of fury, (for you hear his continual prayers on their behalf) but he wishes to deter them and make them more restrained.

But, you say, he upbraided the priest, saying: *God will strike thee, thou whitewashed wall* (Acts 23:3). We are aware that some explain away these words, saying that what he said was prophetic. I do not find fault with those who say this, for that is how it turned out, and how the man died. A more acrimonious critic, prying too deeply into the problem, might in refutation object: If this was a prophecy why should he apologize for what he said, saying: *I did not know that he was the high priest* (Acts 23:5). To this my answer would be that his words were an advice and a warning to be obedient to rulers as Christ was. For Christ, though He had many unutterable things to say of the Scribes and Pharisees, also said: *The Scribes and the Pharisees have sat on the chair of Moses. All things, therefore, that they command you, observe and do* (Mt. 23:2). So here, too, Paul fulfilled the role of prophet and foretold what was going to happen.

If he separated John [5] he did so in the interest of preaching. The one who undertakes this duty cannot be soft or irresolute, but must be strong and vigorous. He should not touch this noble profession if he is not prepared to risk danger and death countless times. Christ Himself says: *If anyone wishes to come after me, let him deny himself, and take up his cross, and follow me* (Mt. 16:24). The one who is not of this disposition betrays many others and would be far better if he stayed silent and kept to himself. Once he ascends the pulpit, he assumes a burden greater than his own powers can sustain, since the salvation of his hearers is at stake as well as his own. It is absurd if a man who does not know how to steer a boat, or how to combat the waves, should not refuse to take the tiller, however many urge him to do so. Yet a preacher embarks on his task aimlessly and haplessly, and undertakes without reflection a task that is akin to countless deaths.

For neither naval pilot, nor wrestler with wild beasts, nor gladiator, needs to be adjusted mentally to death and slaughter as much as the one who undertakes the preaching office. The dangers are greater, the opponents are more formidable, as here slaughter is not concerned with trivia. Heaven is the prize; hell is the penalty for those who lose, the destruction or salvation of the soul. That is the set-up not merely for the preacher of the Gospel but for the ordinary layman, since every man is commanded to take up his cross and follow.

And if every man is so commanded, the preacher and pastor are commanded in a special way, and John who was called Mark belonged to their number. Since he was in the very front line of the conflict, and did not distinguish himself for bravery, he was very properly demoted by Paul, lest his indecision should dispirit the others. If Luke says that there was a contention between them, do not think that this is blameworthy.

To be angry is not sinful, but to be unreasonably angry, without any just cause: *Unjust anger will not be justified* (Sir. 1:28). Therefore, it is not simple, but unjust anger that is censured. Again Christ said: *He who is angry with his brother without cause* (Mt. 5:22), not just simply 'angry'. And the prophet said: *Be angry and sin not* (Ps. 4:5; Ephes. 4:26).

For if anger could not be resorted to, even when the occasion called for it, it would be useless and pointless to have it. But it cannot be pointless, since Providence implanted it in us to correct sinners, to stir up spiritual inertia and sloth, and to arouse the sleepy and indolent. The edge of anger has been given to our mind like an edge of a sword to use it when necessary. Therefore Paul often resorted to anger, and was angry though he loved more than those who spoke gently, doing all things to spread the Gospel as the opportunity presented itself.

Gentleness is not essentially good, but only when the occasion calls for it, so that, if it is not in season, gentleness is unlawful and anger is contumacious.

In saying all this, I am not making any apology for Paul, for he does not need our words: his praise is not from men but from God. [6] My purpose is to instruct my hearers to use the emotions as occasion demands, as I have said already. In this way we can gain merit from every source, sail with great resources into the still harbor, and obtain imperishable crowns, of which may we all be deserving through the grace and mercy of our Lord Jesus Christ, to Whom be glory and power now and always, forever and ever, Amen.

PAUL, A STANDARD-BEARER OF CHRIST

He carried the cross to teach others—His greatness
came partly from God's grace and partly from his cooperation
with grace and his imitation of Christ. His divine call to
the teaching office—His courage, gentleness, and zeal
in the face of every adversity.

The whole population usually turns out when the royal standards are carried in procession, preceded by the resounding trumpet, and escorted by legions of soldiers into the cities. They like to hear the sound of the trumpet, to see the standard carried aloft, and to notice the strength of the standard-bearer. Today at Paul's entry, not into the city but into the world, let us all turn out to watch. For he carries the standard of no mere earthly king, but the cross of Christ, Lord of Heaven. His escort is formed not by mere men, but by angels to honor what he carries and to act as bodyguards for the carrier. If angels are assigned by the God of the universe to those who act in a private capacity without becoming involved in the common welfare, as it is written: the angel who has protected me ever since my youth,[1] much more have they guardian angels who are entrusted with handling the cares of the world and carrying such a load of gifts and such an honor.

Those in the army who are decorated with these honors are dressed in elaborate uniforms, wear golden chains around their necks, and are resplendent in their general appearance. But Paul wears chains instead of golden necklaces, carries a cross, and is hounded, flogged, and starved. Do not be grieved on that score, dearly beloved, for his decoration is better, and more illustrious, and dearer to God. That is why carrying the cross is no burden.

This is the wonder of it, that he is more resplendent in chains, and lashes, and wounds, than if he were dressed in purple and wore a crown. His garments show that he is indeed more resplendent, and that these words are not just empty rhetoric.

Apply to a man smitten with a fever a thousand diadems and purple garments and you cannot make him a whit less feverish. But Paul's rags of garments placed on the bodies of the sick caused their whole illness to vanish, which is only fitting. For if robbers see the standard of the emperor they do not dare to attack but make an about face and take to flight; much more do diseases and devils flee when they see the standard of the cross.

Paul carried this cross not just for himself, but to teach all to do likewise. Therefore he said: *Be imitators of me, after the pattern you have in us* (Phil. 3:17). And again: *What you have seen and heard in me, these things practice* (Phil. 4:9), and again: *For you have been given the favor, not only to believe in him but also to suffer for him* (Phil. 1:29). Human honors usually seem greatest when they meet in the one man. In spiritual matters, on the contrary, honors are more resplendent when many share in them, when they are not narrowly restricted to a single individual, but when many share in enjoying them.

You see, then, that all are standard-bearers of Christ, and that each carries His name before nations and kings. But Paul carried it in the face of hell and everlasting punishment. He did not demand this from others, for they could not endure that much. You see how much virtue human nature is capable of, and that it is man's most precious possession in this life. Can you name me a greater possession? Or an equal one? How many angels and archangels is he not worth who uttered this word? While he was in this mortal and corruptible body, he gave up everything within his power for Christ, and even what was not within his power. For he gave up things present, and things to come, and height and depth, and every other created thing. If this man were in an incorporeal nature, what would he not say? What would he not do?

We marvel at angels because they deserve this honor but not simply because they are incorporeal. Satan is incorporeal and invisible, but no one is more unhappy than he since he offended God who created him. So, too, we call men unhappy, not when we see them in a mortal body but when they fail to use it as they should. For Paul also had a mortal body.

What, then, was the source of his greatness? It was two-fold: partly from God and partly from himself, and what he got from God came because of what he was himself, for God is not a respecter of persons. [3] If you were to say how is it possible to imitate such people, hear what he says: *Be imitators of me as I am of Christ* (1 Cor. 11:1). He imitated Christ. Will you not imitate your fellow slave? He emulated his Master. Will you not emulate your fellow servant? What excuse can you make for yourself?

How did he imitate Him, you ask? Consider his progress from the beginning, from his initiation. As soon as he came from the waters of Baptism, he was so fired with zeal that he did not wait for any teacher. He did not await Peter; he did not come to James, or anyone else, but, directed by his own zeal, he so inflamed the city as to start a violent war against himself. When he was still a Jew he did more than was expected of him, binding, arresting, killing. Likewise Moses, without being ordained for the purpose, assumed the role of defender of his own people against the foreigner.

This is a proof of nobility of soul and generosity of spirit, to refuse to stand by and watch the afflictions of others, even if one has no mandate to relieve them. God showed by ordaining Moses later that he was right to assume leadership. He did this also in the case of Paul. God showed, by quickly introducing him into the dignity of the teaching office, that he was right to assume the role of teaching and preaching at the outset.

If they had assumed the roles merely for the sake of honor and primacy, they could rightly be censured. However, since they loved dangers and courted death in order to save others, who would be so foolish as to censure such zeal?

God's verdict showed that their actions were prompted by a love to save others, as did the destruction of those who loved personal gain. For others assumed rule and leadership, but they were all put to death—some consumed by fire from heaven, others swallowed by the earth.[4] For they acted not in the people's interests but for their own glory. Ozias assumed power but he was condemned and became a leper. [5] Simon Magus [6] assumed power but he was reprobated, and risked being killed. Paul assumed power, but he was crowned not with the priesthood and honors, but with the ministry, and labors, and hazards. Because he started with a great deal of zeal and enthusiasm he was an illustrious preacher from the beginning.

Just as one regularly appointed from the start deserves greater punishments if he does not fulfill his duty properly, so the one who without appointment assumes the office—I do not say of priesthood but of caring for the multitude—and fulfills it worthily, is worthy of every honor. Accordingly, this man, more ardent than fire, did not remain idle for a day, but as soon as he rose from the waters of the baptismal font, kindled a great fire in himself. He did not give a thought to dangers, or the jeers and taunts of his enemies, or their rejection of his message, or any such consideration. He assumed different eyes—I mean those of charity—and another mind, and surged forth with a mighty impetus like a mountain torrent, catching up in his swell the arguments of his adversaries, and showing them Christ through the Scriptures.

Yet he had not at that time many charisms of grace, or an abundance of the Spirit. Nonetheless he was aflame and did everything in a spirit of mortification, as if making satisfaction for his past life. All his deeds were calculated to fortify himself for the battle ahead, filled with dangers and fears.

Although so full of daring and impulsiveness and fire, he always was gentle and amenable to his teachers, and never disobeyed them in the heat of his zeal. For they came and told him in the heat of his zeal, or I should say frenzy, that he should go to Tarsus and Caesarea, and he did not refuse. They said that he should be let down from the wall in a basket, and he agreed. They advised him to shave his head and he did not object. They told him not to enter the theatre and he agreed. His one aim was to undertake everything to help the faithful, and to act in the interests of peace and harmony. He was always prepared to preach the Gospel.

When you hear that he sent his nephew to the tribune, [7] wishing to extricate himself from dangers, that he appealed to Caesar, [8] and that he hastened to Rome, do not think that these are manifestations of cowardice. Would not he who groaned at having to continue in the life here below gladly choose to be with Christ? How could he desire the present when he despised even the heavens and the angels for the sake of Christ?

Why, then, did he act as he did? To continue in his preaching, and to leave this world with many followers, all having won their crowns. His fear was that he would leave life the poorer if he was deprived of the salvation of the multitude. That prompted him to say: *To stay on in the flesh is necessary for your sake* (Phil. 1:24).

Accordingly, when he saw his trial going in his favor, and Festus had said: "This man might

have been set at liberty, if he had not appealed to
Caesar" (Acts 26:32), though he was taken
bound with more chains than those who had committed a host of crimes, he was not ashamed to be
chained in such company. Concerned about the
salvation of all those who were sailing with him,
he was unconcerned about his own safety since
he knew that he would be all right. Taken bound
on such a vast sea, he was as delighted as if he
were being escorted to a mighty empire.

For, in fact, it was no small reward that presented itself to him—the conversion of the city
of Rome. This did not make him overlook a single
soul in the boat. He calmed them, telling them
that he had seen a vision, and assured them that
all who were sailing with him were to be saved. [9]

He did this, not to boast himself, but to make
them receptive toward the Faith. So God allowed
the sea to be moved, that the grace of Paul might
come through what was heard and what was not
heard. For when he gave counsel that they should
not sail they refused to hear him and they encountered extreme dangers. He did not put on
airs because of this, but took every precaution,
like a father caring for his children, lest any of
them should be lost.

When he got to Rome, [10] see how gently he
spoke there, and with what courage he silenced

the criticisms of the infidels. He did not remain there, but continued his course to Spain. [11] He increased in courage in the face of mounting dangers, and became even more daring, not merely himself but also his disciples, because of his example, as, doubtless, they would have been dejected if they saw him yielding and cowering. But when they saw him become increasingly courageous, taking the initiative, and joining issue, they, too, proclaimed the Gospel with confidence. He tells us this in the words: *The greater number of the brethren, gaining courage from my chains, have dared to speak the word of God more freely and without fear* (Phil. 1:14).

If a general is brave, not only when he is slaughtering and laying low, but also when he is wounded, he increases the courage of his subjects, even more so when wounded himself than when inflicting wounds. When those fighting under such a leader see him covered with blood and wounds, but refusing to yield, standing firm, brandishing his spear, shooting at the enemy, and not giving in to his pains, you can be sure that they obey such a leader with all the greater eagerness. This happened in Paul's case. When they saw him bound in chains, preaching even in prison, and overcoming with his words those who had scourged him, they gained greater confi-

dence. So he does not simply say 'they have
dared,' but *They have dared to speak the word
more freely and without fear;* preaching more
courageously, he means, than when I was free of
chains. At that time he also gained more confidence himself. He was more keen-witted against
his enemies, and increasing his punishments only
served to increase his confidence.

In prison he was so overpowering that the
foundations shuddered and the doors flew open,
and the jailer became converted.[12] Even the judge
almost believed, as he himself admitted: *"In a
short while thou wouldst persuade me to become
a Christian"* (Acts 26:28).

Again when he was stoned he entered the
city that stoned him and converted it. [13] They sum-
moned him to trial, at one time his enemies, at
another the Athenians, and his would-be judges
became disciples and his adversaries, subjects.

Just as a fire grows as it catches on to different materials and gains increase from what it
comes in contact with, so the words of Paul converted to himself everybody that encountered
them, and, captivated by these words, those who
warred on him quickly became fuel to this fire
of the Holy Spirit, so that through them the word
spread further and reached others. Accordingly

he said: *I suffer in bonds, but the word of God is not bound* (2 Tim. 2:9).

They frequently put him to flight; they looked like pursuers, but in fact they were prospective followers. The enemy did the work of friends and confederates, never allowing him to remain in one place but keeping the doctor in circulation because of their threats and pursuit, with the result that all heard his words.

They bound him again, but this only sharpened his determination. In driving out his disciples they merely sent them to people who had hitherto no teacher. They led him before a superior tribunal and thus conferred a blessing on a capital city. This made his enemies, peeved with the apostles, say: *"What shall we do with these men?"* (Acts 4:16), meaning our weapons of suppression are their instruments of growth.

They committed him to the jailer to keep him in strict confinement. But the jailer was taken into stricter confinement by Paul. They sent him bound with other prisoners so that he would not escape. But he catechized the prisoners. They sent him by sea, in order to speed a reluctant voyage. But a chance shipwreck made the instruction of his fellow voyagers possible. They heaped up countless punishments on him to extinguish the fire of his preaching. But it continued to spread.

And just as they said of our Lord: *Let us kill him, lest the Romans come and destroy our city and our nation,*[14] and the very opposite happened—because they killed Him the Romans took away their race and their city and what they planned as obstacles actually helped to spread the Gospel—so also in the preaching of Paul. What his enemies calculated to impede the spread of his word only served for its expansion and increased his prestige.

For all these reasons let us give thanks to God Who devises everything for the best. Let us give glory to Paul who made these things possible, and let us pray that we may gain the same blessings, through the grace and loving mercy of our Lord Jesus Christ, through Whom and with Whom be glory to the Father and the Holy Spirit forever and ever, Amen.

SERMON I

[1] cf. Gen. 4:4.
[2] cf. 1 Cor. 15:31.
[3] cf. 2 Cor. 4:10.
[4] cf. Gen. 4:8.
[5] cf. Gen. 6:8-9.
[6] cf. Gen. 8:6.
[7] cf. Gen. 6:14, Ex. 2:3.
[8] cf. Gen. 12:5.
[9] cf. Gen. 26:18.
[10] cf. Gen. 32:28.
[11] cf. Gen. 29:18, 27.
[12] cf. 2 Cor. 11:23 f.
[13] cf. Gen. 39.
[14] cf. Gal. 6:14.
[15] cf. Ex. 32:32.
[16] Mal. 4:5.
[17] cf. Mt. 3:11.
[18] cf. 1 K. 17:1, 2 K. 1:12.
[19] cf. Mt. 3:4.

SERMON II

[1] cf. Rom. 9:3.
[2] cf. Heb. 11:37-38.
[3] cf. 2 Cor. 12:2,4.
[4] cf. Dan. 10:21.

SERMON III

[1] cf. 2 Cor. 11:24 seq.
[2] cf. 2 K. 4:12.
[3] cf. Phlm. 1:10.

[4] Rom. 13:10.

[5] Col. 3:14.

[6] This seems to be a paraphrase of the quotation which follows.

[7] cf. Apoc. 21:6.

SERMON IV

[1] cf. Acts 9:8.

[2] cf. Ex. 32:4.

[3] i.e. Rahab; cf. Jos. 2.

[4] cf. Jon. 3:5.

[5] i.e. Babylas; cf. Chrys. *De S. Babyla* PG. 50. 555. For an account of these related incidents see Baur, *John Chrysostom and His Time* (tr. Sr. M. Gonzaga, Newman Press, Westminster, 1958), 1. 60-69.

[6] i.e. Julian (361-363).

[7] Jovian

[8] Appollonius of Tyana.

[9] cf. Acts 5:36-37.

[10] cf. Ps. 103:22.

[11] i.e. Zeno. But he is clearly thinking of Plato and his *Republic*.

[12] cf. Eph. 6:9.

SERMON V

[1] cf. Eph. 6:12.

[2] cf. Acts 9:23.

[3] cf. 1 Sam. 17:34.

SERMON VI

[1] i.e. Lydia; cf. Acts 16:14, 35-40.

[2] cf. Mt. 26:35.

[3] cf. Gen. 22.

[4] cf. Dan. 3.

[5] cf. Acts 15:38.

[6] cf. Rom. 2:29.

118

SERMON VII

[1] cf. Gen. 48:16.
[2] cf. Acts 19:12.
[3] cf. Acts 10:34, Rom. 2:11.
[4] cf. Numb. 16.
[5] 2 Chron. 26.
[6] Acts 8:18f.
[7] cf. Acts 23:16f.
[8] cf. Acts 25:11.
[9] cf. Acts 27:24.
[10] cf. Acts 19:21.
[11] cf. Rom. 15:24.
[12] cf. Acts 16:25-34.
[13] cf. Acts 14:19-23.
[14] cf. Jn. 11:48.

Index of Scriptural References

THE DAUGHTERS OF ST. PAUL

In Massachusetts
    50 St. Paul's Ave.
      Jamaica Plain
      BOSTON, MASS. 02130
    172 Tremont St.
      BOSTON, MASS. 02111
    381 Dorchester St.
      SO. BOSTON 27, MASS.
    325 Main St.
      FITCHBURG, MASS.

In New York
    78 Fort Place
      STATEN ISLAND 1, N.Y.
    625 East 187th St.
      BRONX, N.Y.
    39 Erie St.
      BUFFALO 2, N.Y.

In Connecticut
    202 Fairfield Ave.
      BRIDGEPORT, CONN.

In Ohio
    141 West Rayen Ave.
      YOUNGSTOWN 3, OHIO

      CLEVELAND, OHIO

In Texas
    114 East Main Plaza
      SAN ANTONIO 5, TEXAS

In California
    1570 Fifth Ave.
      SAN DIEGO 1, CALIF.

In Louisiana
    86 Bolton Ave.
      ALEXANDRIA, LA.

In Florida
    2700 Biscayne Blvd.
      MIAMI 37, FLORIDA

In Canada
    8885 Blvd. Lacordaire
      St. Leonard Deport-Maurice
      MONTREAL, CANADA
    1063 St. Clair Ave. West
      TORONTO, CANADA

In England
    29 Beauchamp Place
      LONDON, S.W. 3, ENGLAND

In India
    Water Field Road—Extension
      Plot N. 143—
      BANDRA, INDIA

In Philippine Islands
    No. 326 Lipa City
      PHILIPPINE ISLANDS

In Australia
    58 Abbotsford Road
      HOMEBUSH N.S.W., AUSTRALIA